# See For Yourself

## Body Science

Catherine Chambers

Published 2009 by
A & C Black Publishers Ltd.
36 Soho Square, London, W1D 3QY
www.acblack.com

ISBN HB 978-1-4081-0855-0
    PB 978-1-4081-1291-5

Series consultant: Gill Matthews
Text copyright © 2009 Catherine Chambers

A CIP catalogue for this book is available from the British Library.

This book is produced using paper that is made from wood grown in managed, sustainable forests. It is natural, renewable and recyclable. The logging and manufacturing processes conform to the environmental regulations of the country of origin.

Produced for A & C Black by Calcium.
Printed and bound in China by C&C Offset Printing Co.

All the internet addresses given in this book were correct at the time of going to press. The author and publishers regret any inconvenience caused if addresses have changed or sites have ceased to exist, but can accept no responsibility for any such changes.

**Acknowledgements**
The publishers would like to thank the following for their kind permission to reproduce their photographs:
**Cover:** Shutterstock: Sebastian Kaulitzki. **Pages:** BananaStock 21; Dreamstime: Imagepointphoto 9b, Sebastian Kaulitzki 6t; Fotolia: Domenico Gelermo 16t, Christian Schütz 13; Istockphoto: Yunus Arakon throughout, Galina Barskaya 4, Julie Masson 17b; Shutterstock: 5t, Oguz Aral 20, Arvind Balaraman 15b, Mario Bruno 19, Felix Casio 5b, Diego Cervo 6b, Lev Dolgachov 16b, Hannamariah/Barbara Helgason 10b, Sebastian Kaulitzki 8, 10t, 11, 12, Julia Lucht 18, Darko Novakovic 15t, Saniphoto 7b.

# Contents

# Body File

Our body parts work together to keep us alive. They help us lead a full life. Many parts rely on each other to work properly. The whole body relies on us to look after it and not to harm it.

## Body under the microscope

### Blood

Takes **oxygen** and **nutrients** around the body.

### Heart

Pump that pushes blood around the body.

### Liver and kidneys

Sort and clean substances in the blood brought from the stomach.

### Lungs

Take oxygen into the blood from the air. Push out **carbon dioxide** into the air from the blood.

### Ear, nose, and throat

Are linked by tubes to the throat. Ears process sounds. Nose processes smells.

### Eyes

Take in and **focus** light. The brain changes it into images.

### Skeleton

Frame of bones. Muscles pull bones to make them move.

### Skin

The body's covering. Helps keep body temperature even.

Scientists often use microscopes to magnify body cells, so that they can be seen.

## A mighty machine

The body has a firm frame of bones and muscles so that we can move around. Inside the body are sets of systems that go round and round. Each system feeds and cleans out different parts of our body day and night.

Exercise helps our body systems to work properly.

# Blood File

Blood is like fuel in a car. Our bodies just cannot run without it. It gives us oxygen, nutrients, and cells that fight disease.

**Plasma**

**Red blood cell**

Blood seen under a microscope showing its four main parts.

## Blood under the microscope

### Plasma

Gooey liquid in which blood cells float. Contains salts, sugars, proteins, **hormones**, and waste matter. Makes up 55 per cent of blood.

### Red blood cells

Carry oxygen from lungs to body tissues.

### White blood cells

Help fight infection and protect against disease.

### Platelets

The smallest blood cells. These group together to form a plug of blood. This helps wounds to stop bleeding.

**White blood cell**

**Platelet**

## Liquid life

Water makes up 78 per cent of blood, while 22 per cent is solids. Each person has from 4 to 6 litres (7 to 10.5 pints) of blood in their body.

# BODY BLOG BODY BLOG B

**READER:**
How do we keep blood healthy?

**BODY BLOGGER:**
We should exercise to keep fresh oxygen in the blood and reduce bad fats in it. Fruit, vegetables, fish, and fresh water help to keep blood healthy.

Some of the foods that help to keep our blood in good condition.

# Heart File

The heart is like an engine. It is a mighty muscle that pumps fresh, rich blood from our lungs to our body. It takes stale blood from our body back to our lungs.

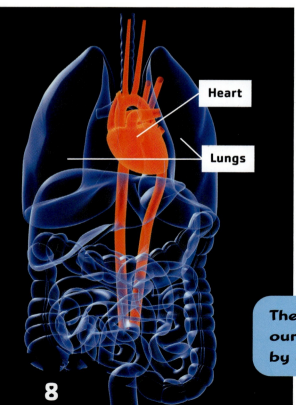

Heart

Lungs

## Heart under the microscope

### Left Atrium

Blood with oxygen flows from this chamber through a **valve** to the left ventricle.

### Left Ventricle

Pumps blood out fast to the aorta.

### Aorta

A tube that takes fresh blood to the body.

### Right Atrium

Blood with carbon dioxide flows from here through a valve to the right ventricle.

### Right Ventricle

Pumps blood out fast to the aorta.

### Aorta

A tube that takes stale blood back to the lungs for more oxygen.

The heart lies between our lungs. It is protected by our rib cage.

**READER:**
My heart sounds like a hailstorm when I run! Why is this?

**BODY BLOGGER:**
Your body needs a lot of oxygen when you run. So the heart pumps oxygen-rich blood quickly around it. And do keep running! Your heart is a muscle and it needs exercise, just like any other muscle.

The heart rate is measured using a stethoscope. It checks if the heart is beating properly.

## Perfect pump

The heart is a red, pear-shaped muscle, about the size of a fist. The heart beats about 60 times a minute when we rest. When we are busy, it can pump twice as fast.

# Liver and Kidneys File

The liver and kidneys are the body's sorting, storing, and waste systems. They are two of the most complicated organs in the body.

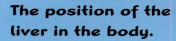

The position of the liver in the body.

## Liver under the microscope

### Lobes

Blood vessels take in nutrients filtered from the stomach. They remove **toxins** that the liver has sorted out.

### Gall bladder

Stores bile juices made in the liver. Bile is released into the stomach to help digest fats.

### Bile duct

Takes bile from the liver to the gall bladder.

## Cleaning tools

The liver is soft, spongy, and dark pink. It is packed with red blood vessels, which filter nutrients and waste. It weighs about 1.8 kg (4 lbs) in a man – the weight of 14 apples. It weighs 1.3 kg (3 lbs) in a woman (10 apples), and it holds about half a litre (1.5 pints) of blood!

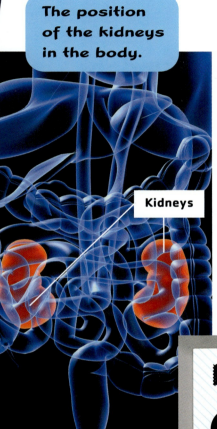

The position of the kidneys in the body.

Kidneys

# Kidneys under the microscope

**Cortex**

Outer layer. Blood has its first filter.

**Medulla**

Inner layer. Blood is filtered more by tiny nephrons.

**Nephrons**

Network of tubes – full of blood or urine.

**Ureter**

Takes urine from kidneys through to the bladder.

# BODY BLOG BODY BLOG

**READER:**
We only have salt-free crisps in the house now. They don't taste the same!

**BODY BLOGGER:**
Kidneys need some salt in order to work. But too much puts a strain on them. Stick to salt-free crisps – you'll soon get used to the taste.

# Lungs File

Without oxygen, there is no life. Our lungs breathe in all the oxygen we need. From the lungs it goes around the whole body. Our lungs breathe out carbon dioxide that we do not need.

## Lungs under the microscope

### Windpipe
Main air tube that connects the throat to the lungs.

### Bronchi
Two tubes leading from the windpipe to the lungs.

### Air tubes
A mass of air tubes leading from the bronchi.

### Alveoli
Air bubbles at the end of the bronchi. They pass oxygen from air tubes into the blood stream.

Windpipe

Lungs

Each tiny air bubble has a very thin wall. Oxygen seeps through the wall into the blood.

## Lungs for life

Lungs have about 300 million tiny air bubbles, which makes them very spongy. The air bubbles are covered in tiny blood vessels, which makes the lungs look pink.

When we rest, we breathe between ten and 18 times each minute. When we exercise, we breathe about 35 times each minute. Our brain tells the lungs when we need to breathe faster.

There is less oxygen in the air at the top of very high mountains. This makes climbing more difficult.

## BODY BLOG BODY BL

**READER:**
Why do I yawn when I am bored?

**BODY BLOGGER:**
When you are bored, your breathing is shallow and you do not take in enough oxygen. Yawning makes you take in a big breath of oxygen-rich air.

# Ear, Nose, and Throat File

Our ears and nose are the doors to smell, taste, and sound. They are connected by tubes from the throat, which is like a highway for the air we breathe.

## Busy body parts

Ears trap **vibrating** waves in the air, which the brain senses as sound. Ears also control balance so that we do not fall over. The nose takes in and filters the air we breathe.

## BODY BLOG BODY BLOG BL

**READER:**
Why do my ears block up when I travel fast uphill or downhill?

**BODY BLOGGER:**
Ears feel blocked when the pressure outside is different from inside the ear. This often happens when you travel high up or low down. Try swallowing to even the pressure

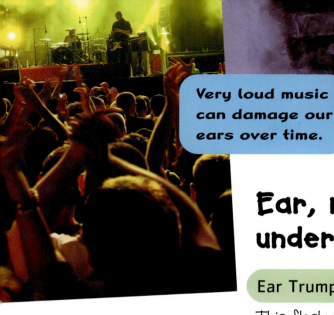

# Ear, nose, and throat under the microscope

Our nose and sinuses produce about 4.4 litres (9 pints) of **mucus** each day. This moistens the mouth, throat, and other body parts.

**Ear Trumpet**

This fleshy cup captures sound.

**Drum**

Vibrates when sound waves hit it.

**Cochlea**

Where vibrations connect to the brain.

**Eustachian tube**

Tube that links ears to the throat.

**Nasal cavity**

Takes in air and smells.

**Vocal cords**

Cords vibrate to make sounds, when air passes from lungs through the throat.

**Tonsils**

Two clumps of soft tissue in the throat. They trap **germs**.

**Epiglottis**

A flap of skin in the throat that directs food into the stomach, not the lungs.

A sneeze can burst from the nose and mouth at 160 km (over 98 miles) per hour.

15

# Eyes File

Eyes are amazing. They take in information from everything around us. This information is light that reflects every object's shape, size, and colour.

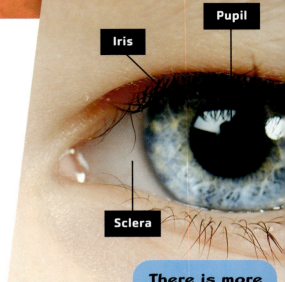

Iris

Pupil

Sclera

There is more to the eye than we can see!

## Eyes under the microscope

### Cornea
Clear coating that helps bend the light onto the lens.

### Lens
Focuses the image onto the back of the eye, like a camera.

### Iris
The coloured part. It opens the pupil wide in the dark to let in more light.

### Pupil
Hole that lets in light to the retina at the back.

### Retina
Picks up light and changes it into messages.

### Optic nerve
Takes the messages to the brain.

### Sclera
Tough case around the eye. Stuffed with soft jelly.

## Magic messages

The eye's curved lens focuses light through the tiny dark pupil. It travels to the retina at the back of the eye. This has nerve endings that change the light into messages. These shoot through the optic nerve to the brain. Here, they are transformed into images. The eye actually receives images upside-down!

## BODY BLOG BODY BLOG B

**READER:**
My eyes are very sensitive to sunlight. Does the colour of the eye make any difference? Mine are a pale grey.

**BODY BLOGGER:**
Yes, the iris has different **pigments**, which protect the eye from too much light. Brown eyes are the best protected as they have more pigment than green, blue, or grey.

Bright sunlight can damage the eyes. Never look straight at the sun.

17

# Skeleton File

The bony skeleton holds the body's organs and brain like a case. It is a frame for our legs and arms, too.

## Holding it all together

We have about 206 bones in our bodies. Some of them are quite bendy, such as our ribs. That is so we can move easily.

Our body has 600 muscles. The brain instructs muscles to **contract** or relax. When they contract they pull our bones where we want them to go. Our muscles only pull. They never push.

## BODY BLOG BODY

**READER:**
I keep pulling my leg muscles when I play sport. But it's only when I am standing around.

**BODY BLOGGER:**
Muscles cool, contract, and tighten when you stand around. Tight muscles pull and tear easily.

A batsman protects bones with padding and a helmet.

# Bones and muscles under the microscope

## Limbs

Arms and legs. The bones are soft on the inside to make them lighter.

## Hip joint

The ball on top of the leg fits into a **socket** in the pelvis. It allows the leg to swivel.

## Knee and elbow joints

Hinge joints that allow limbs to move up and down.

## Ankle joints

Sliding joints that allow feet to move but hold the ankle firm.

## Ligaments

Sliding joints that allow feet to move but hold the ankle firm.

## Tendons

Stretchy bands that tie muscles to limb bone.

## Muscles

Thick bundles of muscle fibres. Packed with tiny nerves and blood vessels.

# Skin File

Skin protects the whole body. It is shower-proof, elastic, and it grows when we grow. What an incredible material! What is more, skin is the body's largest organ.

## Skin under the microscope

### Epidermis

Outer layer of skin made of tough protein called keratin.

### Dermis

Softer inner layer of skin. Has touch, pressure, and pain sensors.

### Hair follicles

Dents in the skin from which hair grows.

### Sweat glands

Three million sacs holding sweat! Sweat seeps out to cool down the body when it is hot.

### Blood vessels

Tiny veins of blood. They narrow in the cold. This stops the heat from blood escaping through the skin.

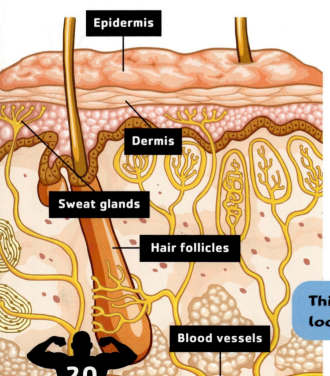

Epidermis

Dermis

Sweat glands

Hair follicles

Blood vessels

This is how our skin looks under its surface.

**READER:**
Why do my fingers go numb when it is cold?

**BODY BLOGGER:**
The nerves at the tips of your fingers start to go numb at about 8°C (46°F). This is because blood stops flowing to your fingertips. The body needs all the blood it can get for vital organs.

## Miracle material

Skin is between 0.5 mm (0.019 inches) and 4 mm (0.15 inches) thick. The thinnest skin is over the eyelids. It is very stretchy so it can move when we blink. The thickest is on the palms of our hands and the soles of our feet. This is so we can hold heavy or rough objects and walk long distances.

In Australia the summers are very hot. Children there learn to always put on sun cream and cover up.

21

# Glossary

**carbon dioxide**  a gas that the body does not use. So, the lungs breathe it out

**contract**  to pull in – in a squeezing motion

**focus**  to concentrate the light from shapes inside the eye. It makes the shapes clearer

**germs**  tiny growing cells that can harm the body

**hormones**  chemicals in the body that affect how parts work or grow

**mucus**  sticky stuff in the nose, throat, and lungs

**nutrients**  tiny amounts of good things that help the body to work

**oxygen**  a gas that the body needs in order to work. Lungs breathe it in

**pigments**  colourings, such as the tints in the skin and eyes

**socket**  a hole made for something to fit into tightly, such as a hip bone in its hip socket

**toxins**  substances that the body reacts to badly

**valve**  a small body part that controls the flow of liquid, or lets it only go one way

**vibrating**  moving backward and forward in very tiny, fast movements

# Further Information

## Websites

A fun website that shows how the body works: **www.kidshealth.org/kid**

Take a tour through the human body at: **www.kidinfo.com/Health/Human_Body.html**

## Books

*The Heart, Lungs and Blood* by Steve Parker. Wayland (2008)

*The Little Encyclopedia of the Human Body by* Richard Walker. Kingfisher (2001)

*The Muscles and Skeletons* by Steve Parker. Wayland (2008)

*What Happens When We Breathe?* by Jacqui Bailey. Wayland (2008)

*What Happens When We Use Our Senses?* by Jacqui Bailey. Wayland (2008)

# Index